# Mrs. Chipley's Chattering Children

## Chianna's Close Call

**Gwen Petreman**
**Illustrated by Andrea Wray**

Order this book online at www.trafford.com
or email orders@trafford.com

Most Trafford titles are also available at major online book retailers.

Printed in the United States of America.

ISBN: 978-1-4907-4922-8 (sc)
      978-1-4907-4921-1 (e)

Trafford rev. 10/25/2014

 www.trafford.com

North America & international
toll-free: 1 888 232 4444 (USA & Canada)
fax: 812 355 4082

Mrs. Chipley had three boys and one girl.

**CHOUNT** loved to count.

From early morning to late at night, he would count everything he saw! He really, really liked to count by

**2's, 5's, and 10's.**

2 , 4 , 6 , 8 , 10 , 12 , 14 , 16 , 18 , 20

5 , 10 , 15 , 20 , 25 , 30 , 35 , 40 , 45 , 50

10, 20, 30, 40, 50, 60, 70, 80, 90, 100

# CHAPE was crazy about shapes.

All he ever talked about were shapes! All day long, he would rhyme off the names of shapes.

# CHEE loved trees.

When he was busy looking for nuts and seeds he would study the trees. His favorite tree was a birch tree. "Want to know why I love birch trees, do you, do you, do you?" asked Chee in an excited voice. "I love birches 'cause they have white bark.

Guess what? Guess what? Guess what? The native who lived here a long time ago used birch bark to make canoes? Want to know why, do you, do you, do you? They used birch bark 'cause it's waterproof. They were smart like me!"

Birch Bark

# CHIANNA loved exploring,

but she had no special interests, like her brothers.
   At this point Chianna reminded Chee, "Nobody wants to listen to a chipmunk who brags. I think it's rather rude!"

   Chianna had barely finished her comment before Chee continued …"Did you know that leaves on trees have millions and millions and millions of hairs on them! Want to know why, do you, do you, do you? The millions and millions and millions of hairs on the leaves trap dust and dirt and nasty pollution!"

Chianna cried, "I guess we're pretty lucky to live in the woods with so many trees! No dirt! No dust! No pollution will ever get into our lungs!"

Usually the four siblings spent their days doing whatever they wanted, but on Saturdays, Mrs. Chipley wanted all of them to spend part of their day playing together.

Today was Saturday. As Mrs. Chipley waved goodbye she reminded the three older brothers to take good care of their younger sister.

As they raced off she could hear Chount chanting:

**1 2 3! Look at me!**
**4 5 6! Jump over sticks!**
**7 8 9 10! Let's count again!**

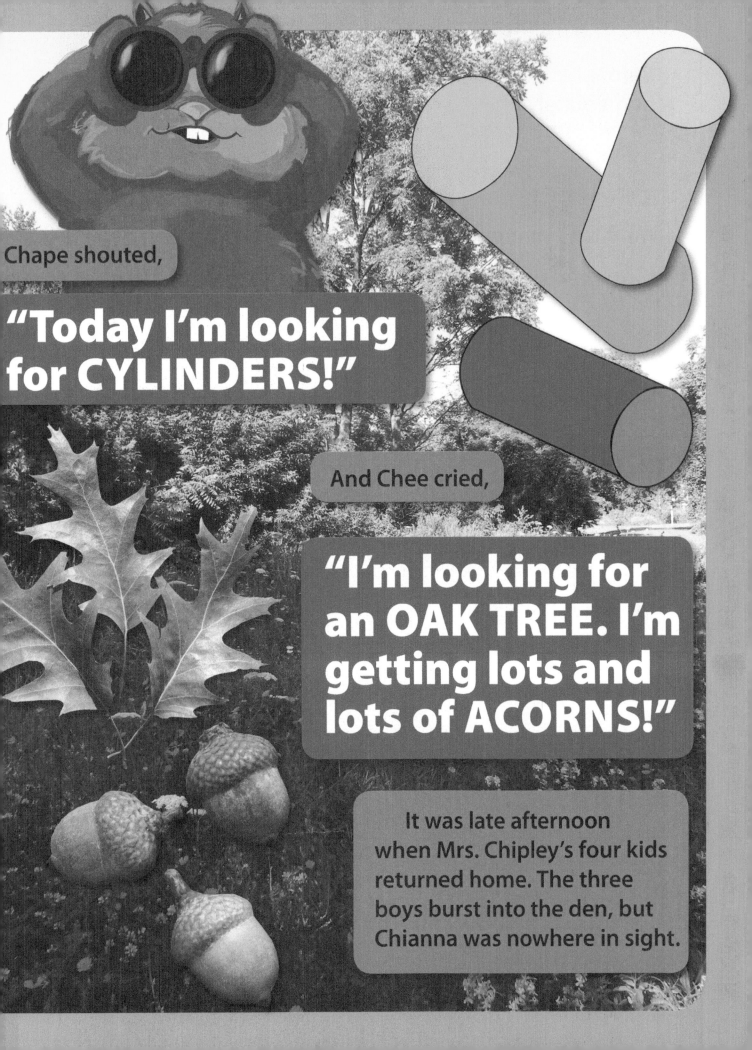

Before Mrs. Chipley could ask about Chianna, Chount immediately blurted out, "Mom! Mom! Mom!

# I counted 100 trees.

Want to hear me count by 2's -

2, 4, 6, 8, 10, 12, 14, 16, 18, 20, 22, 24, 26, 28, 30, 32, 34, 36, 38, 40 ..."

"Okay! I get the picture!" cried Mrs. Chipley. "And, and, and, want to hear me count by 5's?

5, 10, 15, 20, 25, 30, 35, 40, 45, 50, 55, 60, 65, 70, 75, 80, 85, 90, 95 and 100!

And, and, and, want to hear me count by 10's?

10, 20, 30, 40, 50, 60, 70, 80, 90, 100!"

"Could you please, tell me where Chianna ..." before Mrs. Chipley could finish her sentence, Chianna appeared in front of her, dripping with water from head to toe.

"What on Earth happened to you?" asked Mrs. Chipley in a concerned voice.

Cup Plant

Chianna shouted in the loudest voice she could muster "My brothers saved my life!"

"What do you mean they saved your life? From what?" asked Mrs. Chipley.

"Yes! Yes! Yes! We saved her life!" chipped in the three boys in unison.

While Chount was busy counting the leaves on a cup plant, Chape shouted in a loud voice, "I don't believe my eyes!

**The stem on the cup plant is a SQUARE PRISM!** "

"Chee! Stop talking! Chount! Stop talking! Chape! Stop talking!" commanded Mrs. Chipley in a firm voice. "I'm asking for the last time - how did you save Chianna's life?" asked Mrs. Chipley while glaring at her sons.
"Let me tell!" shouted Chape.

## "We used a CYLINDER!

Yup! Yup! Yup! We used a cylinder!"
"What do you mean you used a cylinder?" cried Mrs. Chipley in an exasperated voice.

Chianna finally spoke up, "Never mind, Mom! I'll tell you. While we were playing a game, I accidently fell into a hole. It was really, really deep. I tried and tried to climb out for the longest time. But no matter how hard I tried, I just could not get out! I was so scared. I thought I would never see you again!

"What were your brothers doing when you tumbled into the hole?" asked Mrs. Chipley.

"Oh, I don't know! Chape was busy looking for cylinders. Chount was busy counting everything he saw! They didn't even **notice** that I was missing!" cried Chianna. "I finally shouted as loudly as I could,

## 'I found a cylinder!'

Chape arrived and he declared, 'Chianna, you are right! This hole is in the shape of a cylinder!' "

"How on Earth did you finally get out?" asked Mrs. Chipley in an anxious voice.

"Oh, it was easy, breezy, sneezy, cheesy!" interrupted Chape. "I remembered where I saw a cylinder. So I just got the cylinder and rescued Chianna!"

"**Chape! Listen to me! Right now!** I still don't know how a cylinder got Chianna out of the hole!" cried Mrs. Chipley.

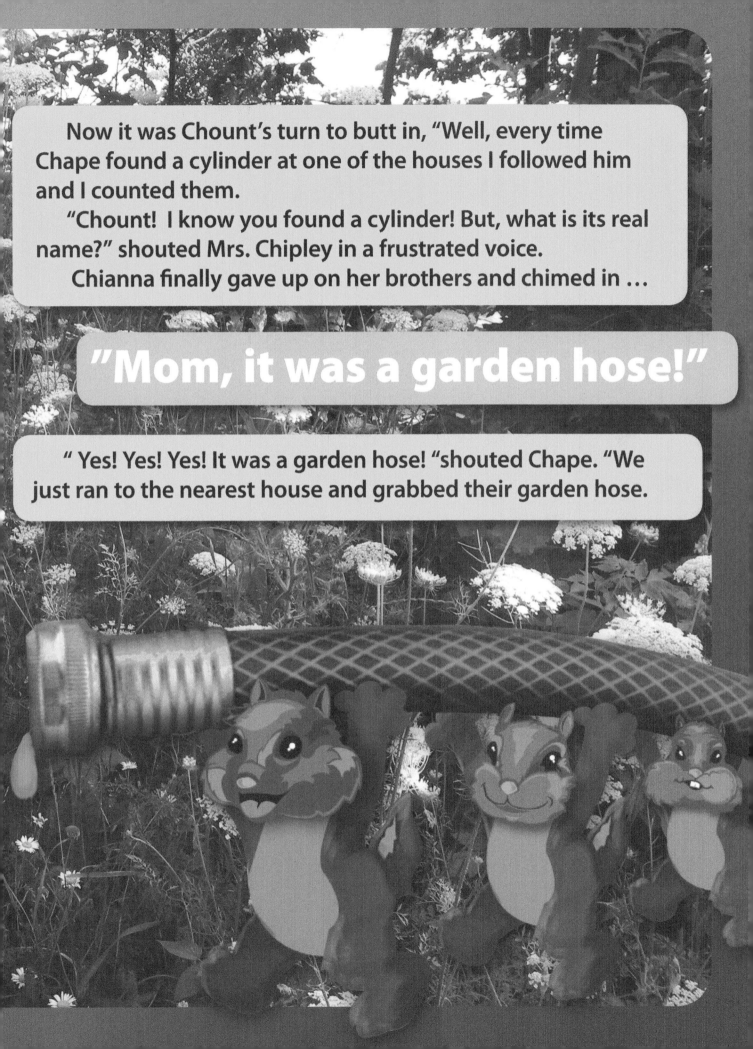

Now it was Chount's turn to butt in, "Well, every time Chape found a cylinder at one of the houses I followed him and I counted them.

"Chount! I know you found a cylinder! But, what is its real name?" shouted Mrs. Chipley in a frustrated voice.

Chianna finally gave up on her brothers and chimed in ...

"Mom, it was a garden hose!"

" Yes! Yes! Yes! It was a garden hose! "shouted Chape. "We just ran to the nearest house and grabbed their garden hose.

But, it was way too long for us to pull! While we were trying to figure out what to do, Chee raced into their backyard to get some acorns from an oak tree. So he helped us pull the garden hose. We pulled and pulled and pulled! We finally got to the hole. Then, we plopped the garden hose into the hole and turned on the water. Presto!

## We told Chianna to TREAD water.

When the water reached the top, Chianna jumped out. Safe and sound!"

"Well, that certainly explains why Chianna is dripping wet, "responded Mrs. Chipley in a relieved voice.

"And Chape, if you had just told me it was a garden hose, I would not have been so confused!" scolded Mrs. Chipley.

"You are not just **one** shape! You are all kinds of shapes!" declared Chape while shaking his head in disbelief.

Chianna started to laugh, "I am a-gone! Get it?" Then she turned around and giggled even more as she declared,

"I am  a-gone! A-gone! A-gone!"

As she quickly sneaked away she could hear Chape muttering to himself while shaking his head, "There are all kinds of polygons! There is a pentagon, a hexagon, a heptagon, an octagon, a nonagon, and a decagon, but I know there is no such shape as an 'a-gone!' "

# Activity Pages

# Queries about Chipmunks

1. How do I identify a chipmunk?
2. Are chipmunks mammals?
3. Where do chipmunks live?
4. What do you chipmunks eat?
5. Do chipmunks hibernate?

## How Many Did You Get Correct?

1. Chipmunks are the smallest members of the squirrel family. They move quickly in spurts of stop and go. They have pudgy cheeks, large, glossy eyes, stripes, and bushy tails. A chipmunk's tail is less bushy than a squirrel's tail. Their cheek pouches allow them to carry several items of food at a time. Chipmunks are solitary creatures and normally ignore one another except during the spring.

2. Yes, chipmunks are mammals. They are warm-blooded. All mammals are born alive except the duck-billed platypus and the spiny anteater. They hatch from eggs. They all get milk from their mothers. They all have hair or fur on their bodies. All mammals have a backbone. And they all breathe with lungs.

3. There are 25 species of chipmunks. They all live in North America except one. They prefer to live where there are trees, shrubs, and rocks. Some chipmunks live in burrows where they make tunnels and chambers. Some tunnels can be about 10 metres (33 feet) long. Other chipmunks make their homes in nests, bushes, or logs.

4. Chipmunks are omnivores which mean they eat plants and animals. They will eat insects, mice, rats, nuts, berries, seeds, fruit, and grain. They can stuff several items of food into their cheek pouches which they carry to their burrows to store for the winter or eat later. Some kinds of chipmunks will eat small birds and small mammals. From April through October, much of a chipmunk's time is spent looking for food. This is referred to as foraging.

5. Chipmunks do hibernate. When the days start to get really cold chipmunks go into their

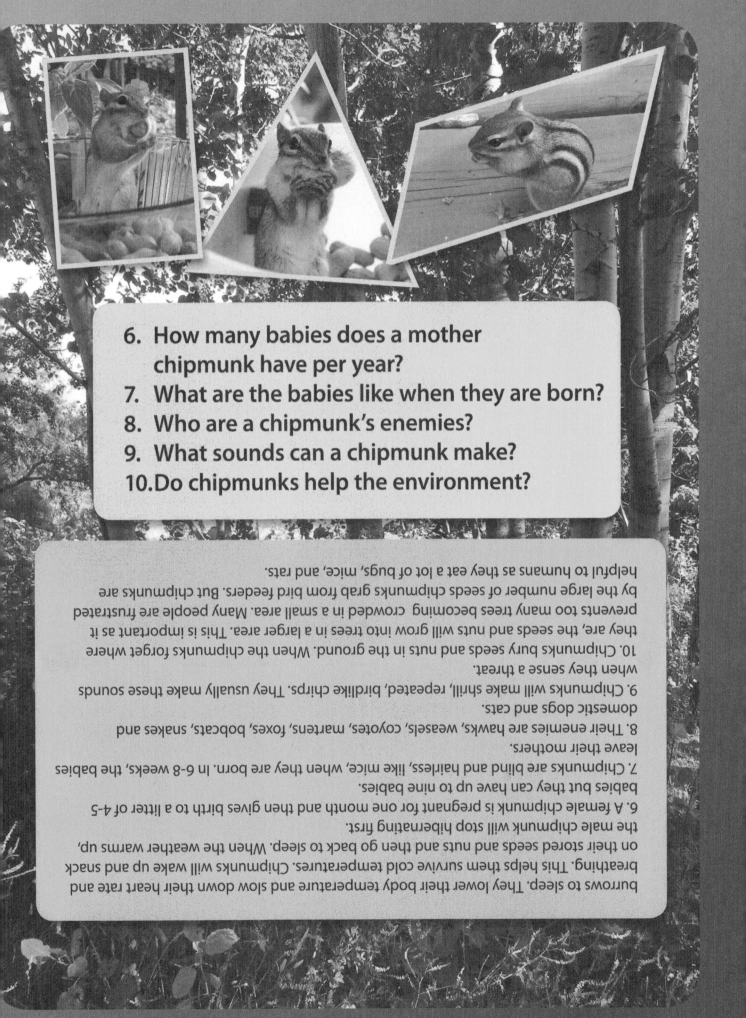

6. How many babies does a mother chipmunk have per year?
7. What are the babies like when they are born?
8. Who are a chipmunk's enemies?
9. What sounds can a chipmunk make?
10. Do chipmunks help the environment?

burrows to sleep. They lower their body temperature and slow down their heart rate and breathing. This helps them survive cold temperatures. Chipmunks will wake up and snack on their stored seeds and nuts and then go back to sleep. When the weather warms up, the male chipmunk will stop hibernating first.

6. A female chipmunk is pregnant for one month and then gives birth to a litter of 4-5 babies but they can have up to nine babies.

7. Chipmunks are blind and hairless, like mice, when they are born. In 6-8 weeks, the babies leave their mothers.

8. Their enemies are hawks, weasels, coyotes, martens, foxes, bobcats, snakes and domestic dogs and cats.

9. Chipmunks will make shrill, repeated, birdlike chirps. They usually make these sounds when they sense a threat.

10. Chipmunks bury seeds and nuts in the ground. When the chipmunks forget where they are, the seeds and nuts will grow into trees in a larger area. This is important as it prevents too many trees becoming crowded in a small area. Many people are frustrated by the large number of seeds chipmunks grab from bird feeders. But chipmunks are helpful to humans as they eat a lot of bugs, mice, and rats.

# Chee's Trees

Chee eats seeds, berries, fruit and grain. He also eats acorns. How did Natives who lived in North America long ago use acorns?

**Answers to Chee's Trees**
For everyday use, the bur oak tree was very important to the native people. The bur oak produced large amounts of acorns every year. The acorn is edible and fairly sweet. If the bur oak grows in limestone areas, the acorn is even sweeter. The natives collected the nuts in bags woven from basswood. They then stored them for the winter in running streams. They were cooked over an open fire. Since they had no salt they improved the flavor with wild herbs. The acorn meat was ground into flour. From the acorn flour, the natives baked a kind of sweet scone called bannock.

# Chape's Shapes

What do you call a polygon that has five fewer sides than a decagon?

**Answer to Chape's Shapes**
A decagon has 10 sides. Ten subtract five is 5. So the answer is a pentagon. A pentagon has 5 sides. "Penta" comes from the Greek language and it means 5.

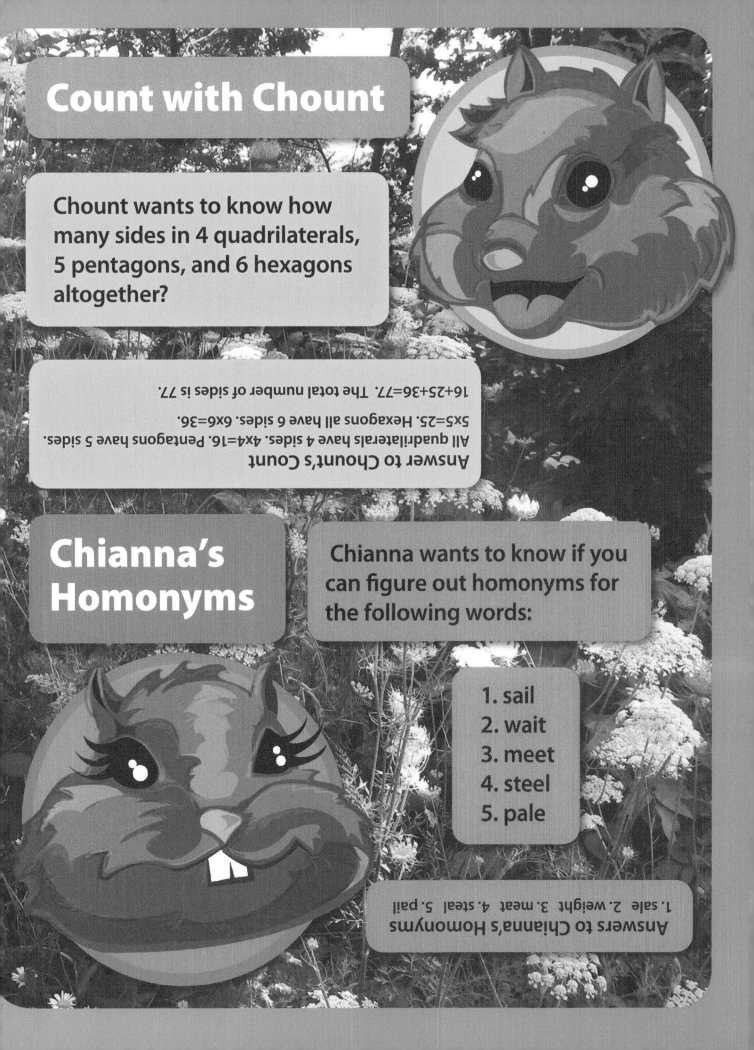

# Count with Chount

Chount wants to know how many sides in 4 quadrilaterals, 5 pentagons, and 6 hexagons altogether?

**Answer to Chount's Count**
All quadrilaterals have 4 sides. 4x4=16. Pentagons have 5 sides. 5x5=25. Hexagons all have 6 sides. 6x6=36. 16+25+36=77. The total number of sides is 77.

# Chianna's Homonyms

Chianna wants to know if you can figure out homonyms for the following words:

1. sail
2. wait
3. meet
4. steel
5. pale

**Answers to Chianna's Homonyms**
1. sale 2. weight 3. meat 4. steal 5. pail

CPSIA information can be obtained at www.ICGtesting.com
Printed in the USA
LVOW02s0453080115

421920LV00003B/6/P

9 781490 749228